First World War
and Army of Occupation
War Diary
France, Belgium and Germany

9 DIVISION
2 Lowland Brigades
Royal Scots (Lothian Regiment)
11th Battalion.
1 April 1919 - 31 October 1919

WO95/1776/9

The Naval & Military Press Ltd
www.nmarchive.com
Published in association with The National Archives

Published by

The Naval & Military Press Ltd

Unit 10 Ridgewood Industrial Park,

Uckfield, East Sussex,

TN22 5QE England

Tel: +44 (0) 1825 749494

www.naval-military-press.com

www.nmarchive.com

This diary has been reprinted in facsimile from the original. Any imperfections are inevitably reproduced and the quality may fall short of modern type and cartographic standards.

© **Crown Copyright**
Images reproduced by permission of The National Archives, London, England, 2015.

Contents

Document type	Place/Title	Date From	Date To
Heading	Lowland (9th) Division 2nd Lowland Bde 11 Bn Royal Scots 1919 Apr-1919 Oct From 27 Bde 9 Div		
War Diary	Haan Germany	01/04/1919	30/06/1919
War Diary	Haan	01/07/1919	09/07/1919
War Diary	StommeIn	10/07/1919	07/08/1919
War Diary	Duren	08/08/1919	31/08/1919
War Diary	Duren Germany	01/09/1919	31/10/1919

LOWLAND (9th) DIVISION

2nd LOWLAND BDE

11 BN ROYAL SCOTS

1919 APR — 1919 OCT

from 27 BDE 9 DIV

WAR DIARY or INTELLIGENCE SUMMARY

Army Form C. 2118

11th Bn The Royal Scots

Place: Maan / Germany

Date April	Hour	Summary of Events and Information
1	0830-1230	A & B Coys on Bn Parade Ground. ½ hour each of P.T., Squad Drill with arms, Squad Drill without arms, Saluting, P.T. 1½ hours musketry
2	0900-1000	C & D Coys under O.C. Coys. 10.00-12.00 Education. Remainder under O.C. Coys. Gymnasium C Coy 0900-1100. D Coy 1100-1200
		Same as for yesterday.
3	0830-1230	A & B Coys on Bn Parade Ground ½ hour each of P.T., Squad Drill with Arms, Squad Drill without arms, Musketry Platoon acting out (1 hr) in Section and Advance to Skirmishing (drill ½ hour) and 1 hour extended order. C & D Coys Same as for 1st.
4		Same as for yesterday.
5	0830-1230	A & B Coys on Bn Parade Ground. ½ hour each of Squad Drill with arms, Squad Drill without arms, Simple field movement, P.T. Extended order 1½ hours musketry. 0900-1045 C & D Coys under O.C. Coys. 1100 Lecture by Lieut Hallam on M.G. distinct 1st Post Bellum Army
6		Divine Services
7	0830-1730	A & B Coys Same as for 5th. 0900-1000 C & D Coys under O.C. Coys. 1000-1200 Education. Remainder under O.C. Coys.
8	0830-1230	A & B Coys on Bn Parade Ground ½ hour each of P.T. Squad Drill with arms. Squad Drill without arms, Extended order Simple field movement. 0900-1000 C & D Coys under O.C. Coys. 1000-1200 Education. Remainder under O.C. Coys.
		Platoon Drill and 1 hour Musketry. 0900-1000 C & D Coys under O.C. Coys. Gymnasium 1000-1200 C Coy. 1100-1200 D Coy
9	0830-1230	A & B Coys. Same as for yesterday. 0900-1000 C & D Coys under O.C. Coys. Remainder under O.C. Coys.
10	0830-1230	A & B Coys on Bn Parade Ground. ½ hour each of P.T. Ceremonial Platoon Drill, Extended order, Musketry, French Advance, 1 hour of Platoon in the Attack. 0900-1000 C & D Coys under O.C. Coys. 1000-1200 Education. Remainder under O.C. Coys. Gymnasium 1000-1100 C Coy 1100-1200 D Coy
11	0830-1230	A & B Coys. Same as for yesterday. C & D Coys same as for yesterday.

Army Form C. 2118.

WAR DIARY
or
INTELLIGENCE SUMMARY. 1/5th Highland Scots
(Erase heading not required.)

Instructions regarding War Diaries and Intelligence Summaries are contained in F. S. Regs., Part II. and the Staff Manual respectively. Title pages will be prepared in manuscript.

Place	Date April	Hour	Summary of Events and Information	Remarks and references to Appendices
	12.		0830-1230 A & B Coys on Bn Parade Ground. ½ hour each of P.T. (1st hour), Musketry (2nd hour), Rifle Exercises, Explanation & Demonstration of the use of Cover v/Ideas in Ground. 1 hour Platoon in Defence. C v D Coys same as A & B. Platoon v. Section in Attack.	
	13.		Divine Service.	
	14.		0830-1230 A Coy P.T. Education and Recreational Training. B Coy ½ hour each of P.T. Ceremonial, Platoon Drill, Musketry, Explanation & Demonstration of the use of Cover & Ideas in Ground. C & D Coys. 0830-1200 P.T. Handling of Arms Musketry Gymnasium. B.F. Separation Recreational Training. March Discipline and 1 hour Platoon in Attack.	
	15.		0830-1230 A Coy on Bn Parade Ground. P.T. Musketry, Rifle Exercises, Platoon in Defence, Explanation and Demonstration of the use of Cover & Ideas in Ground. Application of the use of Cover v/Ideas in Ground. B Coy P.T. and Education. C & D Coys. Route March & Recreational Training.	
	16.		0830-1230 B Coy P.T. and Education. B Coy on Bn Parade Ground. P.T. Musketry, Rifle Exercises, Platoon in Defence, Explanation and Demonstration of the use of Cover and Ideas in Ground. Application of use of Cover v/Ideas in Ground. A Coy. P.T. and B.F. Education and Recreational Training. D Coy. Handling of Arms, Musketry, Gymnasium. B.F. Recreational Training.	
	17.		B Coy P.T. and Education. A Coy Platoon and Section Training, Musketry, Saluting. C Coy P.T., Musketry, Gymnasium, Ceremonial and Recreational Training. D Coy Physical Training & B.F. Education and Recreational Training.	
	18.		Holiday. Divine Service.	
	19.		All Coys 7.30 Kit Inspection and Cleaning of Billets.	
	20.		Divine Service.	
	21.		Holiday.	

Army Form C. 2118.

WAR DIARY
or
INTELLIGENCE SUMMARY.

(Erase heading not required.)

11th Bn. The Royal Scots

Instructions regarding War Diaries and Intelligence Summaries are contained in F.S. Regs., Part II. and the Staff Manual respectively. Title pages will be prepared in manuscript.

Place	Date April	Hour	Summary of Events and Information	Remarks and references to Appendices
Naast	22.		A.Coy P.T. Compulsory Education and Recreational Training. B.Coy P.T. Saluting, Rifle Exercises, Platoon Drill. Guard duties Extended Order Drill and Musketry. C & D Coys Route March and Recreational Training	
Germany	23.		A.Coy P.T. Musketry, Platoon Attacking Strong Post. Rifle Exercises. Platoon shaking out into Action. Skirmishing. Reforming. B.Coy P.T. Compulsory Education. Recreational Training. Outpost Piquet & Sentry Duties. C.Coy P.T. B.F. Education. Recreational Training. D.Coy P.T.B.F. Musketry. Section Platoon Drill. Gym.	
	24.		A.Coy. P.T. Compulsory Education. Recreational Training. B.Coy. P.T. Musketry. Platoon attacking Strong Post. Rifle Exercises. Platoon shaking out into Action. Skirmishing & Reforming. Outpost Piquet & Sentry duties. C.Coy P.T. Musketry. Gymnasium. Ceremonial. Handling of arms. D.Coy P.T.B.F. Education R.T.	
	25.		A.Coy P.T. Musketry Platoon attacking Strong Post. Rifle Exercises. Platoon shaking out in Section. Skirmishing & Reforming. Outpost Piquet and Sentry Duties. B.Coy P.T. Compulsory Education on Recreational Training. C & D Coys Route March and Recreational Training.	
	26.		All Coys as all O.C. Coys on Bn. Parade Ground. P.T.B.F. Musketry & Rifle Exercises.	
	27.		Divine Services	
	28.		A & B Coys in Training Area. 08.30–11.00 P.T. Musketry Rifle Exercises. Platoon attacking Strong Post. Outpost Piquet and Sentry Duties. C & D Coys 07.30–11.00 P.T. Handling of arms Musketry Section & Platoon Drill. 11.00 All Coys HQ Lecture by Lt. Col. Cox – ag 2nd Lond. Bde.	
	29.		A.Coy P.T. Compulsory Education. Recreational Training. B.Coy P.T. Recreational Training. Ceremonial. Platoon Drill. Attacking Strong Post. Rifle Exercises. Platoon shaking out into Section. Skirmishing. Reforming. C & D Coys P.T. Handling of arms. Musketry. Gymnasium & Recreational Training.	
	30.		A.Coy P.T. Musketry. Rifle Exercises. Platoon attacking Strong Post. Platoon shaking out into Section. Skirmishing & Reforming. C & D Coys. Recreational Training. B.Coy P.T. Compulsory Education. Recreational Training. C & D Coys. P.T. and B.F. Education. Recreational Training. Platoon Section Drill.	

R.N. Allan Capt
11th Bn Royal Scots

Capt 11th Bn Royal Scots

Army Form C. 2118.

WAR DIARY
of
INTELLIGENCE SUMMARY.
(Erase heading not required.)

M.G.C.
11th Bn. The Royal Scots.

May 1919

Place	Date	Hour	Summary of Events and Information	Remarks and references to Appendices
HAAN	1st		"C" Coy P.T. + Compulsory Education. Remedial training "B" Coy Training as per 5th day of 3rd week.	
GERMANY	2nd		"C" Coy as per Coy training programme. "B" Coy under O.C. Coy.	
	3rd		"A" Coy as per Training programme. 5th day 3rd week. "B" Coy P.T. (compulsory Education & Remedial training "C" Coy) O.C. Coy.	
	4th		Bn Church Parade as possible. C.O.'s Inspection. "A" Coy Minded "C" Coy with rifle + kit.	
	5th		Parade. Divine Service.	
	6th		Parade as per Bn Training Programme	
	7th		" " " " "	
	8th		" " " " "	
	9th		" " " " "	
	10th		Bn Kit Inspection. "B" Coy Relieves "A" Coy in the outpost line.	
	11th		Divine Service.	
	12th		As per Bn Training Programme	
	13th		" " " " "	
	14th		" Each Coy athletes & trials for a trip on the Rhine.	
	15th		" Lecture. On "Swimming after the War".	

Army Form C. 2118.

WAR DIARY
or
INTELLIGENCE SUMMARY.

Place: Malta
Unit: 1/4th The Royal Scots
Month: May 1919

Place	Date	Hour	Summary of Events and Information	Remarks and references to Appendices
MARA	16		The G.O.C Malta D.N. Maj Gen Sir H.K. Butler KCMG. CB inspected the Bn.	
GERMANY	17		Kit Inspection under OC Coys. A Coy relieves B Coy in the outpost line.	
	18		Divine Service.	
	19		Parades as per Bn training programme.	
	20		B. Route March. Shoni Inf. 8 fn. Coy.	
	21		Parades as per Bn training programme.	
	22		Wiring Bn continues work, the Afyanini position.	
	23			
	24		Kit Inspection. B Coy relieves A Coy in the outpost line.	
	25		Divine Service.	
	26		Parades as per Bn training programme.	
	27			
	28		Usual O.C. Coys inspection of billets.	
	29		As per Bn training programme.	
	30		Parades as per Bn training programme. A Coy on Tanahui Range. G.O.C Salonika this visits near climbs	
	31		Inspection. C.O. Inspects an outpost. A Coy relieves B Coy in the outpost line.	

S. Aumgester
A/Lt 11 Bn The Royal Scots

11th R Scots
9.0 Louvroil
Louvain

Army Form C. 2118.

WAR DIARY
or
INTELLIGENCE SUMMARY.
(Erase heading not required.)

Place	Date	Hour	Summary of Events and Information	Remarks and references to Appendices
Noon Germany	June 1		Divine Services	
	2		A Coy PT BF Education Pool Shooting. B Coy Musketry Infantry Training. Arm Drill. Baths. C Coy Education. Range. Recreational Training. D Coy Musketry Education	
	3		A Coy Musketry Infantry Training Baths. B Coy PT BF Education. Pool Shooting. C Coy Rifle Range Education	
	4		D Coy Miniature Range and Recreational Training	
	5		All Coys under O.C. Coys for Musketry, Infantry Training and Arm Drill. Recreational Training	
	6		A Coy Miniature Range & Recreational Training. B Coy Musketry Education. C Coy PT BF Education & Baths. D Coy Musketry Infantry Training Arm Drill & Pool Shooting	
	7		A Coy Musketry Education. B Coy Miniature Range Recreational Training. C Coy Musketry Infantry Training. D Coy PT BF Education Baths	
	8		Arm Drill Pool Shooting. D Coy PT BF Education	
	9		A. B Coys Kit Bullet Inspections. C Coy PT BF Bullet Inspection. D Coy Musketry. D Coy relieves A Coy on Outpost Line.	
			Divine Services	
	10		A Coy PT BF Rifle Grenade Practice Baths. B Coy Minden Ob Coy Arm Drill & Education. C Coy Rifle Grenade Practice & Education	
	11		A Coy Rhine Units. B Coy PT BF Rifle Grenade Practice Baths. C Coy PT BF Education	
	12		A Coy Education. Gas Test. Recreational Training. B Coy Rifle Grenade Practice (Live). C Coy Gas Hut Baths. D Coy Education	

Army Form C. 2118.

WAR DIARY
or
INTELLIGENCE SUMMARY.
(Erase heading not required.)

Instructions regarding War Diaries and Intelligence Summaries are contained in F. S. Regs., Part II. and the Staff Manual respectively. Title pages will be prepared in manuscript.

Place	Date	Hour	Summary of Events and Information	Remarks and references to Appendices
Maas	12		A Coy Rifle Grenade Practice (cont) B Coy Coy Excavation + Gas C Coy Working Party D Coy Gas Excavation + Baths	
Vermony	13		A Coy under O.C. Coy. Excavation. B Coy Working Party + E Coy Rifle Grenade Practice (cont)	
	14		A Coy Working Party B Coy Inspection of Billets + Kits by Commany Officer C Coy relieves D Coy in Outposts	
	15		Divine Services	
	16		A Coy Range Application 200 J.D.ea B Coy Lewis Gun Training C Coy under O.C. Coy Rifle Grenade Practice.	
			D Coy under O.C. Coy Gas Test.	
	17		A Coy Lewis Gun Training B Coy Application 200 J.D.ea 3 rounds for Coy Sniper at Railway Bridge K.840.875. M.9.676 M.9.173.	
	18		A Coy P.T. B.F. Training under O.C. Coy B Coy Lewis Gun Training C Coy under O.C. Coy's for Training D Coy P.T. B.F. Excavation	
	19		A Coy under O.C. Coy Drill. B Coy - Coy Drill under O.C. Coy C Coy under O.C. Coy Training D Coy Range Application J.D.	
			D Coy relieves Hy in B Pln for the Outposts F.L.	
	20		A Coy Ceremonial. O.C. Boys Inspection B Coy P.T. B.F. Training under O.C. Coy C Coy Ceremonial under O.C. Coy D Coy P.T. B.F. Ceremonial.	
	21		A Coy Lewis Gun Training B Coy Ceremonial. Inspection by O.C. Coy's D Coy relieves C Coy in the Outpost Line.	
	22		Divine Services	
	23		A Coy Range Application 200 J.D. ea B Coy Lewis Gun Training C Coy mar O.C. Coy Rifle Grenade Practice D Coy	
			under O.C. Bat Training	
	24		A Coy Lewis Gun Training B Coy Range Application 200 J.D. ea C Coy under O.C. Bat Training D Coy P.T. B.F. Excavation	
	25		A Coy Lewis Gun Training B Coy Lewis Gun Training C Coy Lewis Gun Training D Coy P.T. B.F. Excavation	

WAR DIARY
or
INTELLIGENCE SUMMARY.

(Erase heading not required.)

Army Form C. 2118.

Place	Date	Hour	Summary of Events and Information	Remarks and references to Appendices
Huam	26		A Coy under O.C. Coy to Coy drill. B Coy Lectures near O.C. Coy. C Coy Work OC Coy Lecture	
Germany	27		D Coy Range Approx 200 X D.O.	
			Company Officers Games. All Coys	
			A Coy PT R.H. Training under O.C. Coy. B Coy Command Depots by OC Coy. C Coy & D Coy now	
	28		O.C. Coys to Training. Supervised by O.C. Coys	
	29		Divine Service	
	30		A Coy Range 100 yards Application. B Coy Bayt Training. C Coy Guard post to as Racing	
			Bridges K.840.875. K.86.76. K.84.43. Outpost find taken over from 11 Welch by D Coy	

Major
Commanding 11th The Royal Scots

WAR DIARY or INTELLIGENCE SUMMARY

Army Form C. 2118.

Place	Date	Hour	Summary of Events and Information	Remarks and references to Appendices
Alaan	Aug. 1		A Coy Training Platoon & Coy Drill. B Coy Range 200 yds Appl. F.D. C Coy Outpost. D Coy P.T. & Education.	
	2		B.F. & Education. B Coy P.T. and Education. C Coy Outpost. D Coy Training	
	3		P.T. & Education. Ceremonial, Specialist Training C Coy Outpost D Coy B.F. Education	
	4		Ceremonial Specialist Training including Bombing. B Coy B.F. Education. C Coy Outpost. D Coy Musketry Swimming	
			Test K.R. Para 11-13.	
	5		A Coy Training K.7.8. B Coy Training g.K.7.8. C Coy Outpost. D Coy under O.C. Coy for Training.	
	6		Divine Services	
	7		A Coy Range 200 yds appl. I.D. B Coy Training g.K.7.8. C Coy Outpost. D Coy under O.C. Coy for Training	
	8		Training K.7.8. B Coy Range 200 yards Appl. I.D. C Coy Outpost - relieved by 12 K.R.R. D Coy P.T. Education	
	9		Battalion moved to STOMMELN.	
STOMMELN	10			
	11	0900-1100	Battalion Cleaning Billets, reorganizing kits and interior economy generally. All Coys under O.C. Coys for inspection & drill. 1000-1200 Cleaning kits organizing etc.	
	12		All Coys under O.C. Coys for Cleaning kits, reorganising and interior economy generally.	
	13		Divine Services	
	14		All Coys under O.C. Coys for P.T. B.F. rapid loading 0830-0930. 0930-1230 A Coy Baucator. B Coy Range. C Coy Baths. D Coy Coy Pack Racing	
	15	0830-0930	B.F. Coys under O.C. Coys for P.T. B.F. rapid loading. 0930-1230 C Coy Education D Coy Range. A Coy Coy Football Party	

Army Form C. 2118.

WAR DIARY
or
INTELLIGENCE SUMMARY.
(Erase heading not required.)

Instructions regarding War Diaries and Intelligence Summaries are contained in F. S. Regs., Part II. and the Staff Manual respectively. Title pages will be prepared in manuscript.

Place	Date July	Hour	Summary of Events and Information	Remarks and references to Appendices
STOHLEN	16.		A & D Coy on Training 0830-0930 B Coy 0830-0930 under O.B. Coy P.T. R.F. Rapid loading 0930-1230 Education C Coy Bayonet fighting.	
	17.		0830-0930 A+B Coy P.T. B.F. Rapid loading 0930-1230 A Coy Education. B Coy Ceremonial Meeting C+D Coy Tactical march.	
	18.		A Coy 30° Range Meeting B Coy Training 0830-0930 C Coy P.T. B.F. Game 0930-1230 Spring Drill Coy Drill Ceremonial	
	19.		08.30-0930 D Coy P.T. B.F. rapid loading 09.30-1230 Education	
			0830-0930 All Coys P.T. Games 0930-1230 Interior Economy	
	20.		Divine Services	
	21.		A Coy 0830-0930 P.T. B.F. Rapid loading 0930-1230 Education. B Coy 0830-0930 P.T. B.F. etc 0930-1230 30° range C Coy Training and	
			Baths. A Coy 0830-0930 P.T. B.F. Rapid loading 0930-1230 Coy Ceremonial Drill Musketry	
	22.		A Coy Baths. A+B Coy Route march. 0830-0930 C Coy P.T. B.F. Rifle loading 0930-1230 Education. D Coy 0830-0930 1000-1130 Range	
	23.		A Coy Training B Coy 0830-0930 P.T. B.F. rapid loading 0930-1230 Education Baths C Coy Range and musketry D Coy Training	
	24.		A Coy 0830-0930 P.T. B.F. Rapid loading 0930-1230 Education B Coy 0830-0930 P.T. Musa 0930-1230 Spring Coy Drill Ceremonial C+D Coy Field march.	
	25.		A Coy 30° Range Musketry B Coy Training C Coy 0830-0930 P.T. B.F. Rapid loading 0930-1230 Spring Coy Drill Ceremonial D Coy 0830-0930 P.T. B.F. Rapid loading 0930-10 Trench.	
	26.		All Coys Interior Economy	
	27.		Divine Services	
	28.		0930-1100 hours Cleaning Billets. 11.00 Sports	
	29.		Comman Off. to Chief Inspectia Conferm at. A Coy Annual Musa Rings B Coy Bayonet Training C Coy training D Coy P.T.	

(19175) Wt W2358/P260. 60,000. 12/17. D. D. & L. Sch. 52a. Forms/C2118/13.

Army Form C. 2118.

WAR DIARY
or
INTELLIGENCE SUMMARY.

(Erase heading not required.)

Instructions regarding War Diaries and Intelligence Summaries are contained in F. S. Regs., Part II. and the Staff Manual respectively. Title pages will be prepared in manuscript.

Place	Date	Hour	Summary of Events and Information	Remarks and references to Appendices
STANDEN	July 30.		Inspection of Arms. Remainder of day Sports.	
	31.		" " " " " " "	

A.A. Oakly Lieut Col.
Commanding 1/5 The Royal Scots

Army Form C. 2118.

WAR DIARY
or
INTELLIGENCE SUMMARY.

(Erase heading not required.)

An April 1919   1st Bn. The Royal Scots

Place	Date	Hour	Summary of Events and Information	Remarks and references to Appendices
STOTTMEN	Aug 1		Battalion Orders.	
	2		A & B Coys. Inspection of Arms. Lecture by Rev. J.H. Hewart B.A. C & D Coys. Football. All ranks Whole Holiday.	
	3		Divine Services.	
	4		A Coy. B.F. Education Baths. B Coy. Range (Rifle & Lewis Gun) Bombing. Gas training. C Coy. P.T. Education. D Coy. Outpost Scheme.	
	5		A Coy. Outpost Scheme. B Coy. B.F. Education Baths. C Coy. Musketry Range. Rifle Lewis Gun. Bombing. D Coy. P.T. Education.	
	6		Battalion Route march.	
	7		Move to DÜREN. A & C Coys to Teveren. B & D Coys to Barracks.	
Düren	8		Battalion reorganising billets duties.	
	9		Guards Working parties and pickets. A Coy moves to Barracks.	
	10		Divine Services.	
	11		Guards Working parties and pickets.	
	12		do	
	13		do	
	14		Guards Working parties and pickets. All available men under O.C. Coys Inspection. Gas drill.	
	15		do	
	16		do	

Army Form C. 2118.

WAR DIARY
or
INTELLIGENCE SUMMARY. No. 10.

(Erase heading not required.)

Place	Date	Hour	Summary of Events and Information	Remarks and references to Appendices
Duren	Aug 17		Divine Service. Awards	
	18		Under O.C Coys Kit Inspection	
	19		Inspection by B.G.C. 2nd Inf Bde. Awards	
	20		All Coys Physical Training 0900-1000. 10.30-12.30 All Coys Bayonet. D'of mt inspect. Barrack	
	21		D Coy at Aufrob of O.C. Coys for general overhaul. Remands of boys under OC Coys Inspection for training Concln	
	22		A Coy under OC Coys for Rifle + overhauling. Remainder under OC Coys P.T.R.F Education. Handing over by C.O on meeting of Bn. + kit Extra	
	23		0900-1000 All Coys P.T and B.F. 1030-12.30 Whole Bn. Coy of Coy training Manners, Kit Inspection	
	24		Divine Service	
	25		Best Kent March. D Coy Guards and visiting tactics	
	26		A Coy P.T Bayonet. B Coy B.F Education. C Coy P.T Bayonet. D Coy B.F and Concln	
	27		A Coy Drills and Ceremony. B Coy Baths + Education. C Coy P.T + Education. D Coy P.T. Baths	
	28		0900-12.30 A + C Coys Handling of Arms Musketry. 10.30-12.30 B Coy Education B Coy hunting. D Coy Coy Training	
	29		A + C Coys Coy training. B + D Coys Handling of Arms Goo. Musketry and concln.	
	30		Under OC Coys Cleaning of Guards School Coy of Kit Inspection 4.O. a transport Baths	
	31		Divine Service	

H.L George Col. A.S.C
11th Bn. M.C. Royal Scots.

WAR DIARY or INTELLIGENCE SUMMARY

Army Form C. 2118.

(Erase heading not required.)

11th S- The Royal Scots

September

Place	Date	Hour	Summary of Events and Information	Remarks and references to Appendices
DURSET	1st		B. Ronli: Jack him fighting over Rifle Milet.	B.Coy. Inan Jugget DURSET
GERFAPT	2nd		J.T.B.I. Evacuation	" " " "
	3rd		Rifle Range. Evacuation Batt: Specie Welpol Polant	" " " "
	4th		Trans. hip. 9 Am. Mackay. Ga. Evacuation.	" " " "
	5th		At ochool 9 ar. Coyo	
	6th		R.S.M. Lanes. O.C. Coyo Specia	B Coy Macend by 6 N.O.R.S
	7th		Divini Service	
	8th		2.S., 3rd Class Army Educ.n Examination	
	9th		0900-1000 O.C. Coyo Infantri. Tr. S.B.	110th Int Arto
	10th		Rifle Range. Evacuation Batt:	
	11th		" Ga. Mackay. B. Coy. training	
	12th		An C. Coyo training. 3rd D. Coyo Ga. Mackay. Evacuatn	
	13th		R.S.M. Lanes. O.C. Coyo Specia. Same	
	14th		Divini Service.	
	15th		B. Ronli Jack oor fighting n.R. Salonan.	
	16th		" Evacuatin 9 hours. war Shrine Army Rifle meeting	

Army Form C. 2118.

WAR DIARY
or
INTELLIGENCE SUMMARY.
(Erase heading not required.)

September 1918 11th Royal Scots.

Instructions regarding War Diaries and Intelligence Summaries are contained in F. S. Regs., Part II. and the Staff Manual respectively. Title pages will be prepared in manuscript.

Place	Date	Hour	Summary of Events and Information	Remarks and references to Appendices
DURET	17th		Rifle Range. Baths. Recreation.	
GERMANY	18th		3 to 10 Coys training. Rly Coys. Hackin. Gu. Rifle Grenades.	
	19th		All Coys training unit orders.	
	20th		RSM's Parade. Unit orders.	
	21st		Divine Service.	
	22nd		General Bording Instructions. Inoculation.	
	23rd		"	
	24th		"	
	25th		"	
	26th		"	
	27th		"	
	28th		Divine Service.	
	29th		Graves. Bathing. Parties.	
	30		" " "	

J. N. Cunningham Capt.
11th Royal Scots.

Army Form C. 2118.

WAR DIARY
or
INTELLIGENCE SUMMARY.
(Erase heading not required.)

War 11th B" The Royal Fus:
October

Instructions regarding War Diaries and Intelligence
Summaries are contained in F. S. Regs., Part II.
and the Staff Manual respectively. Title pages
will be prepared in manuscript.

Place	Date	Hour	Summary of Events and Information	Remarks and references to Appendices
DÜREN	1st		P.T. B.F. L.Gun Class. Signaling Class. Education. N.C.O.s men R.S.M. Batt.	
GERMANY	2nd		" Batt.	
	3rd		" Batt.	
	4th		P.T. B.F. Commanding Officer kit Inspection. N.C.O.s men R.S.M.	
	5th		Divine Service. Kits Evening. Clay Pigeon Shoot	
	6th		Lewis Gunners on the Range. Musketry P.T. B.F. Signaling Class. Education.	
	7th		P.T. B.F. Lewis Gun & Signaling Classes. Education.	
	8th		" " N.C.O.s men R.S.M.	
	9th		" "	
	10th		" "	
	11th		" O.C. Coys Inspection. Cleaning of Barracks. Clay Pigeon Shoot by Col Royal Fus: & Don Jaget	
	12th		Divine Service.	
	13th		L.Guns on Range. P.T. B.F. Signaling Class. Education. N.C.O.s men R.S.M.	
	14th		Bn Route March. Lewis Gun Lighting Drill. Barracks	
	15th		L.Gun & Signaling Classes. Education. N.C.O. men R.S.M.	
	16th		" Batts	

Army Form C. 2118.

WAR DIARY
or
INTELLIGENCE SUMMARY.
(Erase heading not required.)

1/5 Loyal R.

Instructions regarding War Diaries and Intelligence Summaries are contained in F. S. Regs., Part II. and the Staff Manual respectively. Title pages will be prepared in manuscript.

Month October

Place	Date	Hour	Summary of Events and Information	Remarks and references to Appendices
DUREN	17		Union octrofo	
GERMANY	18		S.T. Divine Service	
	19		Divine Service	
	20		S.T. one coy. Parades	
	21		"	
	22		"	
	23		"	
	24		"	
	25		All available NCO's men transfers from 5/6 Royal Lks. to 1. 1/5 Loyal Lks. 5 by Inn. August	"
	26		Divine Service	"
	27		Reorganization	"
	28		Reorganization	"
	29		Inter. one coy.	"
	30		"	"
	31		"	"

J.S. Ainsworth Lt Col.
1/5 The Loyal Lks.

www.ingramcontent.com/pod-product-compliance
Lightning Source LLC
Chambersburg PA
CBHW081509160426
43193CB00014B/2637